Six Lips

Six Lips

Penelope Scambly Schott

Mayapple Press 2009

© Copyright 2009 by Penelope Scambly Schott

Published by   MAYAPPLE PRESS
408 N. Lincoln St.
Bay City, MI 48708
www.mayapplepress.com

ISBN 978-0-932412-84-3

ACKNOWLEDGMENTS

Alhambra Poetry Calendar: "Kisses and Kisses"; *Arroyo*: "Second Tour" and "Now that I live among the baboons,"; *Canary*: "Among the Other Animals"; *Cider Press Review*: "Landscape with Grandson"; *Earth's Daughters*: "Ghost Lovers"; *Eclectica*: "Spring Housecleaning"; *Ginosko*: "There is one thing that is close and one thing that is far"; *MO: Writings from the River*: "Compass" and "Snakes"; *Naugatuck River Review*: "How I Scare Myself": *Nimrod*: "Poor Dear"; *The Rambler*: "My Hard East Coast Heart: The Wife's Story"; *Rhino*: "In Which I Am the Skeleton Girl" and "As If I Could Ever Go Home"; *Thresholds*: "Here's How I Used to Make Myself Cry"; *Umbrella*: "Eclipse"; *US 1 Worksheets*: "The Long Russian Movie of My Life" and "So let me tell you,"; *VoiceCatcher*: "Counting the Body"

Also, some of these poems were read on the KBOO radio station in Portland, Oregon.

Cover art by Melinda Fellini. Cover designed by Judith Kerman.
Book designed and typeset by Amee Schmidt with titles in Pristina and text in Adobe Caslon Pro.

Contents

I

Compass	5
Snakes	6
Among the Other Animals	7
Self-Portrait as a Horse	8
How We All Came to Survive	9
My Obituary	10
Can't you do anything right?	11
How I Scare Myself	12
Preparing for the Tea Party	14
Here's How I Used to Make Myself Cry	15
The Shawl Store	16
The Shadow Life	18
Inside a house of dying	19
In Which I Am the Skeleton Girl	20
My Hard East Coast Heart: The Wife's Story	21
Kisses and Kisses	22
Poor Dear	23
Ghost Lovers	24
Why I Do Not Wish to Float in Space	25
Second Tour	26
The Men in the Other Room	27
There is one thing that is close and one thing that is far	28
The shadow	29
The Long Russian Movie of My Life	30
Outline for a Sexual Biography	31
I Tried to Explain the World to My Sister	34
After the Yellow Jackets	35
Marriage Manual	36
Now that I live among the baboons,	37
Landscape with Grandson	38
Bouquet	39
Behind the Waterfall I Become Invisible Again	40
The Eyes of Fever	41

II

Counting the Body 45

III

Heart Failure 53
Spring Housecleaning 55
What I Got 56
My Hobo Heart 57
As If I Could Ever Go Home 58
The UN Commission on Refugees: A Radio Interview 60
Incidental Music for the 6:00 pm News 61
A Question of Class 62
So let me tell you, ... 63
Moral Accounting: A Song Cycle 64
Malingering in the Cellar of Grief 68
How Do I Grieve for You? 69
Eclipse 70
Daily Phone Call to My Mother 71
How Death Intends to Instruct 72
I am pregnant with my mother's death 73
Riding to Lluriac 74
A Woman Painter 75
In the Voice of My Mother Who Wants to Die Faster 76
Key 77
Understory 78
Sacrament of the Moths 79

*For Rebecca and Adele, daughters of my heart,
may I be gentle with you always*

I

Compass

I left in the East a canal full of turtles,
hedgerows of roses and Osage orange;

I hid in the West a cardboard box:
ashes of a dog who crossed her paws;

I mislaid in the South the black balaclava
that made me look like a stick-up man;

up in the North I forever abandoned
the hooded anorak of innocent fur.

I lost in the Past my ability to remember;
I rummage the Now for the gift to forget.

My scant mother is old and shriveling;
soon earth & sky will belong to the Future:

the day she dies I'll get drunk as a duck,
and I'll mark the night with a white stone—

this one, the same damn pebble
I keep hoarding for Truth

in the wet cupboard of my mouth.

Snakes

The hopes of snakes are mostly horizontal,
twisty in grassland and wise beyond their skins.

Snakes dream under rocks until sunlight splotches
the June meadow, yellow and blue, and clouds

cast hot shadows. In this meadow I stand dreaming
of the man at the bank, how he lured me into the vault

where I wept for the lack of money. Always my children
were busy outgrowing their shoes. Always my children

drank all the milk. Ate all the biscuits. The snakes
are sunning their ripples in slow streaks. The snakes

are ribbons splayed in the pages of my old cookbook.
Its spine is cracked, its pages stained with butter.

I love to caress the scales of snakes. They feel
like expensive leather. Almost as good as paying

my whole electric bill at once.

Among the Other Animals

Please excuse me as I carry this leg-waving beetle
out to the yard and watch it go.

Surely it values its walking to and fro upon the earth
as I value my own.

Sometimes I envy the salmon who knows how to go
back to the river in which it hatched.

I have been at sea a long time and am sniffing
my way home. This is the estuary

where the test of selfhood is not words or tools
nor any ability to anticipate death.

Nights when I answer the screech owl, music vibrates
the back of my throat,

a language half known: a Spanish speaker almost
understanding Portuguese,

until I become one in the common clan of beasts,
the animal itself, akin to kin.

Self-Portrait as a Horse

A bear with scimitar claws
is shredding the clouds
into white tatters.

A sun-lit jet glints and thrums.
Silver pylons patrol the river.
Berries harden on canes.

Behind the hedge gap, a mare
rears up. Her haunches
are scarlet leaves.

On this November hill, nostrils
flare. The red mare gallops
in my raiment of flesh.

How We All Came to Survive

1.

Now, in my house of one thousand paintings,
I salt my soup with the dust of colored chalk.

I have bright green fingertips
like ten live spirits in ten forest robes.

My fingers are flowing with green
like a woman who suckles ten children.

Now my children have grown tall as trees.

2.

There once was a young woman stuck in a tree.
Below her, the animals all sat at table.

Even back then,
she always knew better than to mention out loud

the boiling of various bones—*bones, oh, bones, oh*—
in a tin pot with a pinhole, and steam scalding

her poor thummy-thumb-thumb.

3.

Mama.   Baby.
Baby.   Mama.

We are raising our thumbs to summon
babies and beasts in their variegated stripes:

fang, claw, hawk in the peach tree, each rising
in the bright thicket of its kind.

I am kissing my painterly thumb
to salute this life.

My Obituary

will be Chapter One in my second life.
As for the funeral, I don't plan to attend.

And now my life starts to get interesting.
First I get born on a mountain summit.

The glacier stamps my right foot blue.
I wear the mark for this whole next life.

I learn how to dance inside a crevasse
where I mate with a mountain goat.

I spell out my words in yellow lichen
while my kids grow long white fur.

This frozen life, I can promise you,
is the wisest of lives I have chosen.

For a last life, I will hatch in a lake.
My name may be Polliwog, Duffel

of Mysteries. Or Smoothed Rock.
Biography makes for honest work.

Can't you do anything right?

she asks me.
My thumbs grasp my twisted purple umbilicus,
holding on.

The sectioned placenta
drapes over my shoulders like a pink cape.
I'm all dressed up to go home.

In my next birth,
I shall arrive with a golden garden snail
over each miniature thumb.

She will say:
Thank you, Sweetheart. I shall sleep softly
in my breakable shell.

Child, she will whisper,
you delight me.

The stalks of my antennae
will rise in the air, their black eyespots
fixed on her dry lips.

How I Scare Myself

Hey, you there, grab another chocolate truffle
from this tarnished silver dish.

Nobody in my father's house ever admitted
the fetish of matter, the lucidity of lace.
My mother muttered the beauty of mending.
No one declared the importance of butter,
its sheen on the satin drapes of desire.

When I smashed up the village of childhood,
I arose from the rubble a dangerous woman.

I squatted in a corn field among diagonals of silk,
and I spoke out loud the names of the devils:
the devil-of-despair,
the devil-of-regret,
the devil-of-expecting-apologies.

I summoned those devils out of the hedgerows
and smashed in their heads with my hoe.

A chocolate, a brandy, a love affair, a fair shot at survival:
the good girls are groveling between wooden pews,
the good girls are marching single file over the widening
isthmus of wrinkled skin,
the good girls are weeping into their plastic laundry baskets.

Shush. Finish sucking chocolate off of your teeth.
Don't think you can guess how this story ends.

Anything you ask from me now will be on fire:
flame from my mouth,
flame from my forked beard,
flame from the tips of my calloused fingers squeezing

death's neck.

Listen.
Hiss of a jeweled snake: SCORCH.

Preparing for the Tea Party

I've powdered my welcoming face with dust
of my ex-husband's heart, because and because

all the designers who advertise in the *New Yorker*
are arriving by limousine to tour my home.

This shriveled eel was my lover's penis;
I'll store it in the hassock where I hide my tail.

This tea chest is made from cedar of Lebanon;
the knob on the chest is a knuckle of Saint Jude.

Around my grandmother's lion-footed table,
the bunch of us will sip at our tea—

my finger, crooked through a Limoges handle,
soon to display its long and tapered nail.

I've turned the dog's poultry-flavored toothpaste
French-side up: *Goût de volaille.*

At last I have become completely exquisite.
I hope you are watching;

I hope you will tell my mother.

Here's How I Used to Make Myself Cry

The little white ceramic horse
who came in a tea box and didn't whinny.

The way the tape measure snapped
its yellow tongue back into its square shell.

Not to mention the giant pinking shears
shutting those angry zigzag teeth.

I hid like a spy in the high attic dormer
as the neighbor opened her dollhouse door.

How nobody in the world knew I was there,
how the warm inner crook of my elbow

tasted like honeysuckle,
how I held myself in my own arms.

The Shawl Store

1. Green Velvet Shawl

Sometimes, on rainy afternoons,
   I rub my shawl against my cheek—
      one harbor seal rafting up to another.

To be touchable on all my skin
  as if water could clasp the flesh,
     to go stepping out through the rain.

Softness. The privilege of belonging.
   The compact flaring of bear grass,
      its tart smell on my hands.

Why would I shiver? Why would I weep?
   My green velvet shawl. Green shawl.

2. Black Feather Shawl

Yes, I am elegant: iridescence flapping on a twig.
When I show up as a crow, please don't be shocked;
you see, the truth is I have always been a crow.
Truth is, there's no such bird as the truth.
Truth is, I'm a flaming liar. See how this soot
has soiled my heart? Beauty lies in the eyes
of the beholden is what they don't say.

3. Invisible Shawl

The shoemaker's daughter arrives in grass sandals,
the fisherman's daughter wears overlapping scales,

the poet's daughter is clothed in disclosure,
the crow's chicks in featherless pink skin.

The cedars are tricked out in licorice ferns
and strands of old-man's-beard. Only I

am naked. Today I am wearing
the glamorous air.

The Shadow Life

When you dream in the house of stairs,
you can creep down to the cellar
where the pale mother of moths
is powdering her silver wings.

When you dream in the house of stairs,
you can mount up to the tower
where bright splinters of sun motes
are striping the wide floorboards.

When you sleep in the house of stairs,
you must crouch between two landings
where a shabby Sibyl under the bed
is stuffing long fingers into holes.

When you sleepwalk inside that house,
you have misplaced your twin feet
and can step neither up nor down,
can breathe neither in nor out.

When you wake in the house of stairs,
there are skulls nailed to the newel posts,
golden birds perched on the banisters;
birds chime the chord of your spine.

Inside a house of dying

there hides a blue cloud
indistinguishable from sky

The old woman in the bed
is neither rushed nor slow

Her children in the kitchen
tell stories over tea

The voices needn't be so
hushed

because the dying woman
is no longer listening

Through unmoving eyes
she watches the cloud:

nothing else in the room
is that warm
                or that close

In Which I Am the Skeleton Girl

A girl collects a world of broken knuckles and totes
them home in her shawl.

She toes the down in the wood duck's nest, a fluff
she used to love to label *loving-sacrifice*.

Two birds sing from the aspen, but not to each other
and not to me.

A jet lifts over the coast range to the wide Pacific.
I am riding its contrail west as I swivel

my head in the six known directions of earthly unrest.
You may call me *Owl*.

Call me *She-who-once-believed-in-justice*. Or this:
Owl-without-hands-to-save-us.

My Hard East Coast Heart: The Wife's Story

We were moving to the West.
We were busy arguing
about which stuff to bring
and which stuff to throw out.

He was listening to the radio.
I was making more boxes.
He heard it on the radio
so he turned on the television.

I was taping boxes.
He watched the second jet hit.
I was stacking boxes.
Everything fell down.

I kept on piling up boxes. After
it happened and kept re-happening,
he wouldn't throw anything away.
I said, *You'll use any excuse*,

but there weren't any excuses;
I had packed up my heart
in bubble wrap and trucked it
mountain ranges away.

Kisses and Kisses

On this night of the highest tide, mice skitter
over the glinting track, tails swishing like sweepers.

When the last trolley arrives, I ride to the island
where the man who swore he would wait

has already left. I swathe my face in ivory chiffon
until the moon through gauze smells of burnt sugar.

Feral cats, black as licorice, slink among dunes.
Kisses and kisses. Fur sticks to my wet and craving

tongue. This isn't the first time love has gone wrong.
Girls, let me tell you, I could have done worse.

Poor Dear

*I don't like penises
very much*, she said.
*It's life with a two-year-old:
ME, ME.*

*You're trying to cook
or sleep or read,
and here's Sir Penis
plump with need,*

*poking the folds
of your skirt, whopping
your leg, begging.
Men are okay,*

she said, *but penises
make me tired.
It's the stare
I don't care for,*

*that one glistening
eye. Thank God
I don't have one
except by marriage.*

*Imagine the drag:
trailing it around
like some third leg
or a mailing tube*

*packed with explosives,
a dumb joke.*
But he looked so sad,
her heart broke.

Aw, Sweetie, she said,
*I didn't mean it—
what I just said,*
and took him to bed.

Ghost Lovers

White chiffon blouses in a thrift shop,
their hangers tangled

shoes drumming the raised boardwalk
in a summer town

arms and legs swinging in rhythm

On a seventh wave, the beautiful dead
ride in

you stagger out from the sea, clutching
one transparent crab

foam slides down your legs

I offer you my stack of faded towels
with stripes or appliquéd fish

And now on baked sand, your shadow
covers my shadow

imagine the rubbery bull-whip kelp
stroking our skin

how its tough bulb
contains all the air we need

Why I Do Not Wish to Float in Space

Who cradled a body to fit this maple chair?
Who shaped a lap to prop a dog's chin?
Who spread the western horizon to snip

the orange sun in half?

      Was it the flesh,
the eye, the I, the blatant contact between
thing and thing, a warm humming of flesh,
swell of rock against my back?

Can you feel how our planet spins in a void,
how the shallow mantle, hauling its fur coat
of forest, its slippery skin of ocean, seems
inconsequential over the molten core?

I've lost my footing in the belly of curled roots,
and I'm scared of falling, of lurching clear out
into space—nothing on earth to touch. Pull me
back by a finger, will you?

Please?
Here, in the motionless house, my face
brushed by your glance.

Second Tour

While my husband packed to fly back to Vietnam,
this time as a tourist instead of a soldier,

I drove to the zoo to say goodbye to the musk oxen
who were being shipped out early next morning

to Tacoma. We were getting lions instead.
When I got there, it was too easy to park.

The zoo was closing early so they wouldn't let me in.
I went back to my car and slid into the driver's seat.

Sobs tore from deep in my chest, I who had never
seen a musk ox and never cared until now.

The Men in the Other Room

The two men are watching a funny movie.
They don't discuss fathers or their old war.

Later they'll crank up pressure washers
to de-moss their separate driveways,

but now the men are sharing one couch
and their deep giggles are adorable.

The men in the other room are not young;
their bellies strain their shirt buttons.

Yes, each one belongs to a woman:
mine is the old silver-back on the right.

Would he be vexed by what I'm writing?
Am I *Objectifying*? I call it *Blessing*.

There is one thing that is close and one thing that is far

and that one thing is the sky stretching above sight as I breathe
fragments of sky into my throat as we kiss at the curb as the brush
edges of your mustache prickle my open lips as we press so close
that this goodbye kiss will fly east with me across the whole broad
continent more present than the cracked badlands or square fields
or winking rivers between tiny trees, and how our kiss, like starlight,
is the one thing that is close and the one thing that is far

The shadow

of the leaf is more engrossing than the leaf:
moment after a kiss, moment before a murder.
Nothing has come of nothing and won't,

or hasn't yet. Now I imagine I sent
the president a sonnet and the president
sent me a gun. I would dandle

the gun in my lap, like a baby
or a map or a glass basin for augury
or the slimy net I found by the pond.

We are all candle-wasters under the sun.
Whatever a tadpole learns from a frog,
the tadpole is bound to forget.

I think tadpoles think about water
in the same way I thought about time,
testing my fresh feet. I thought

that story plots made sense, like a peony
or a symphony or sympathy or the blinking
and perforated shadow

of one leaf of the copper beech,
wide-branched beech tree where I turned
gold illuminated pages. It was summer,

it was always summer. Only Abe Lincoln
had ever been shot. The sun set late.
My sister and I never got old.

The Long Russian Movie of My Life

I might as well wear my dead aunt's fur cloche
and the long-haired wrap with tails at both ends.

The sleek winter wolves are tracking the carriage,
and I'd rather be mouthed by wolves than breathe
the popcorn gone rancid with train-oil my cineplex
uses for butter. How I wanted to fling myself under
the wheels, to turn into a dime flattened on steel,
to rest hot and thin above shattered glass,
that glitter of diamonds and brown and green.

Don't go down by the tracks, said my grandmother,
where men do things to girls, but mostly it seemed
like they spat and peed, which was much less scary
than some of the men I would end up marrying,
or the raw night I squatted in weeds by the siding
because it was safer than going home.

Always the perfume of creosote,
always the tall black engine approaching,
the eye of the headlamp growing enormous.

Outline for a Sexual Biography

A. The Genital Child

1. Soap

Pink perfumed heart in a cellophane box.
I plopped it into the tub and scrubbed,
everywhere.

The soap stung. There.
Skin within the skin.

2. Hassock

My sister and I
roll on the hassock,
squishing our juicy insides.

Mommy arrives to scold us both:
You're too old.

B. Primary Education

1. Field Trip

I liked to diaper little baby boys:
giblets and neck but a lot smaller.

2. Elementary Vocabulary

What is
Adultery?

It sounds so totally
grown up.

3. Intermediate Vocabulary

When I heard
there was a word

   masturbate

I was astounded
others had found it.

4. Advanced Vocabulary

Nuts and rocks. Prick and dick.
Cunt and beaver. Diddle and frig.

Spit swap. French kiss.
Cun.ni.lin'gus. Yuck.

C. Applied Research

1. Losing It

Gosh, it was tedious:
always a wrong boy
in a wrong place.

No joy,
to say the least.
And the least said...

2. She Gets Around

She'd cook for a soft look.
She'd undress for a caress.

Hell, she'd lie with the Devil
and grovel for His approval.

3. Mr. Vodka Is Incontinent

Once, when she was half asleep,
it came upon her over the water
of dreaming,
            all of her,
from her head to her feet,
lifted
     into a single billowing
wave,
but when she was fully
awake, she was holding her pillow,
and his side of the bed
was drunk-pissed wet.

4. Mr. Sexy

He flirts for hours, thinks he's fetching:
lascivious glance, innuendo, tentative
stroke, three short pokes.
Poof. It's over.

D. Gospel

1. Sunday Morning Sex

We fit every time, your basic pair
of old shoes.

We are falling below the national average,
savagery of need relieved
by regular use.

Let's hear it for Old Shoes.

2. The Best News

That body and mind are one.
That one and one are sometimes one.

That the mind in the groin
can shut words down.

I Tried to Explain the World to My Sister

At night she coughed. Days, she asked questions.
I was three years older and thought I should know:
which bits are the gumbos in chicken gumbo soup?
What I didn't know, I improvised. My explanations
seemed reasonable, my delivery authoritative:
our hard breast bones will pop out into breasts.

Or oddities: alternate cosmos of a cactus garden
where whatever looked wooly was sharp, thorns
blossoming to giant asparagus. Or ocean lore:
the wet translucence of moon jellyfish flapping
and closing like pink valves of the heart. As if
by teaching my sister the world, I could hold her

in it. Unlikely that she and I will depart this life
together in matching patent leather party shoes.
Baby sister, bury my child-eyes under the earth
where I can study root causes. So sweet, sweet,
the lies I told you; now as I weep in the garden,
don't let me capsize this argosy of brown snails.

After the Yellow Jackets

1.

I stepped into a nest. Thirty angry yellow jackets
stung. I burned in bed for a week. My face swelled
into hot lumps. The room turned dark, light, dark.

My dog jumped on and off the bed. The moon grew.
I lay there, missing my first dog. We used to crawl
under barbed wire fences. The young, I thought,

can't know how beautiful they are. Later
I would say to the check-out girl at Kroger's,
You are so beautiful. She chomped her gum.

Strung barbed wire cast such brilliant shadows.
Since the stings, I always want to fly into sunrise,
crossing water between sea foam and moon.

2.

My father died on an island just before dawn,
after a good night's sleep. His blotched hands
lay open and loose on a summer sheet. The room

grew lustrous. Maybe I've described this before.
Daddy, it's time to stop writing about you. I need
to explain things in different words:

>   As if kindness is my dog's wet tongue on clover
>   with no fierce bees. Or how beyond us that morning,

>   the ocean shone like a bending field.

Marriage Manual

Begin slowly: unzip my boots. Run your fingertips
over my ankle. Now lift your face; a last streak of sunset
is cracking the clouds. See those golden treetops?

No, I told you, don't mess with the breasts.

Pull off my boots. Roll down my socks and ball them together.
Now tell me something you remember out of childhood,
a playground story or a grade school teacher's name.

Please, not the crotch either. Not yet.

Run your thumb under my arch. Yes.
Whisper to me about music or your first dog. I am almost ready
to smell your neck, to unbutton your shirt. I love your earlobes

and the curve of your bottom lip. Now kiss me slowly
and just this softly. All around us, the clouds are flaming.

Now that I live among the baboons,

a black river divides days from days. It floats away
what I have failed to do.

The black river mocks my housekeeping. Hooligan baboons
leap crocodile to log.

They swipe the ripest fruit along the bank. Often they pelt me
with seeds and husks.

The river doesn't remember my father. The dreams it carries
are rudderless.

And yet I discover,
as it flows past baboons on its prodigal way home,

that this living river
travels freighted with stars.

Landscape with Grandson

A squirrel unlatches the slats of the pinecone
Seeds throb in humus like tiny clocks

A human child tips his perfectly shaped skull
to watch the sun cross the blue arch

Hide these words in your tight back pocket:
squirrel   pine   boy   sky

Bouquet

1.

Bare-armed among daisies, rowing, nearly drowning,
perfume of soured milk, sweetness of child sweat,

to braid the edged stems, a first escape from home

2.

The rose remembers the bud,
the bottle remembers the cork,
the cookbook, its red silk cord—
the cord too short to hang myself,
bottle too empty to poison myself,
the rose with black-spot mildew.

> The man at the railroad station
> standing among wooden benches,
> how I lusted; the woman I was
> who went in.

3.

Jasmine steam, warm curve of the tea mug;
big white dog sprawled on my lap, her curly legs
across my knees, rump flopped over my thighs.

Extension: remote sail gone under the horizon;
silence after wind.

4.

Chinese lantern flower
pulsing like an orange coal,
lighthouse with a Fresnel lens
rotating its beam over the lawn,
gray people, extinguished,
dead stars moving around.

All of them, I have been all
at the great gathering-in.

Behind the Waterfall I Become Invisible Again

— *Silver Falls, Oregon*

White water spilling over
the basalt lip of a cliff,
mist rising,

waist high ferns
damp as rain beginning
over and over.

I went there, and there
I rejoiced wildly.
At that place was no Eye.

A waterfall spinning
its wide veil.
Or the dim vestibule

of the vagina,
the original blind place.
How far in can you go

and still come back?
As if I have seen *Being*
become *Is*.

The Eyes of Fever

Sometimes I crave the eyes of fever,
  every color sharp, the lines distinct,
    strands of the waterfall weaving together,
      the shapeliness of thought.

I would like to be permanently gifted
  with the acuity of convalescence,
    to dwell at the edges of getting well,
      to wait like a horse or a mountain.

If I were newly returned to my life,
  I would love each tendon of my wrists,
    like pulling at the tendon of a chicken foot
      to close its yellow and elegant claws.

How to live in this state of rawness?
  Somewhere directions scratched on a wall?
    Or maybe it happens only in your final illness
      as you convalesce from being alive.

"

Counting the Body

1. One Tail, Please

Is a tail too much to ask?
But I care what kind. Nothing stumpy.
A great feathery plume. A gorgeous tail.
A glorious flag of a tail, happily visible
over the hedges.

Yes, you can bet I'll be wagging it,
just like my dog
wags her own golden-and-white appendage.
And I'll gladly cut tail-holes
in all my best clothes.

This is no trivial promise:
my grandmother taught me the button-hole stitch.
I sat on her porch and practiced until my thread
didn't tangle.
Then I could ride my bike,

a second-hand Schwinn I named Black Beauty.
Sometimes the bicycle was the horse
and sometimes I was the horse.
Fast and wild, we circled the block, pedaled
past neighbors until they all disappeared.

We galloped into that secret place,
our manes and magnificent tails
flying out backwards,
wind from some faraway sea
trembling in our turned ears.

2. On the night I have two vaginas,

I will try to discover two shy men
who cannot admit they love men.

I'll invite them both into my bed
and guide them each to embed

a veined penis in a wet vagina,
each man mindless of vaginas

but both touching my open body
so closely they believe the body

they touch is flesh of one another.
Treasure my gift. I offer no other.

3. The Uses of Three Ears

My left ear listens only to truth.
The right records what's false.

A bird chimes. Also a clock.
One of them lies.

Now ask me about my third ear.
It listens best. It lurks

under my left breast to hear
what risks coming true:

   this is a blood journey,
   your lover forgets you,
   and the dog is dead

4. Woman with Four Tongues

First is my tongue of fire. It singes the wind.
Kings and scholars cover their eyes.

Next is a tongue of honey. Furred with bees
and the shadows of bees, my honied tongue

hums in the meadows. My third is the tongue
of infinite silence. It is the wisest.

And the last is my tongue of snow. Flakes
melt as it touches the sky.

When my sister and I were tiny girls,
we stood in the back hall

tongue to tongue. It was always icky
and we always kept trying it.

Now all my four tongues are thirsting to lick
the closed lids of your eyes.

First, feel my tongue of fire.

5. The Well-Armed Five-Armed Woman

Five elbows sound just about right. I'll roar
down tight corridors, I won't be shoved aside.

There's no way five elbows can fold in tight
to my girlish waist. I plan on using up space,

as much space as a man takes. I'll strut
elbows akimbo, jutting out in crowds. Also

I'll employ that fifth elbow behind my spine,
but my best elbows are these poking forward

out of my chest, this set of magnificent spikes
like twin damascene weapons, pointy, bony,

so much sharper than breasts.

6. Six Lips

Six lips to sip the sublime,
   two for the mouth and four for the vulva,
      plump as succulents and shining with dew—
         ah, youth; ah, time.

7. If I had seven eyes,

I would look east and west
with my yellow eye and my red eye;

I would see sunrise and sunset,
I would follow the beaver scarring the pond
at dusk.

With my white eye and my green eye,
I would look north and south;

I would watch the she-bear licking her twins
as their lumpen muzzles nuzzle her teats.

With my brown eye and my blue eye,
I would peer down and up:

worms turning soil under the roots,
and one hawk over an open field
where mice run in tunnels of grass.

With my seventh eye, the blind eye,
I would look inward:

I would study my own soul—
how it intends to keep living forever

but shrinks down to the size of an eye
and blinks shut.

8. Brooding Giantess

Across the lake lives a vast giantess
with eight arms and eight huge armpits.

Under each one of her warm armpits,
the giantess broods a different egg.

One of them is sky blue
like pieces of hope cooped up inside it.

A second rattles with unspent bullets.
A third roars like a discordant horn.

Another is stuffed with single mittens,
each mitten mislaid by a child.

The fifth encloses false promises
made by lovers, one to another.

The sixth contains numerous deaths
planned ahead for the new year.

And the seventh, a spotted egg,
contains all the pain in the world.

Which of these seven eggs will hatch?
Don't ask, says the giantess,

*but the eighth, a tiny off-white egg,
a hummingbird with no green feathers*

*yet, that one will hatch out well.
Its beak will enter deep wells of nectar.*

9. These Are My Nine Knees

On two knees I bow down to spring;
my knees get wet in the new mud.

On two more I worship summer,
the luxuriance of flower and stalk.

On all fours I praise autumn
and its singing harvest of gourds.

And on my very last leg, I balance
in snow, begging each girl or woman

I ever tried to be. But none, not one,
will bless me or my nine old knees.

10. If I Had Ten Thumbs

I would wear pink leather shoes with velcro straps
I would strike matches on the sole of my shoe
I would suck firmly on my ten wet thumbs
I would practice exactly how to suck
with rapt attention and rhythm
so as to gratify any man
and I would do it
yes I would
do that
yes
and

                              afterwards
                       although my lips
               might forever remember
          sucking the muzzle of a pistol
       I would practice whispering *Sister*
    I would reach out to those warm hands
reaching toward mine and I would chant *ahh!*
like ten ancient abbesses on ten ineffable islands
with ten joyous and toothless mouths I would smile

∭

Heart Failure

1.

This is the year I would like to find pity. I would like
to hurt for my mother the way I ache for my children
whenever anything major goes wrong in their lives.
I want to feel vicariously glamorous when she models
the umber cashmere sweater she bought half-price
in the overpriced boutique by her favorite sushi shop.
I would like to gasp for breath whenever she grabs
for her oxygen tube and jiggles the prongs into sore
nostrils. I want to tremble and feel confused
when she can't retrieve e-mail messages and starts
to panic. When her skeletal legs burn under sheets,
I wish my own hard-muscled calves would throb.

I want to be sad that she's eighty-seven and fading.
I want to invent memories of how she encouraged me
when I was a child, how she helped me when I
was a young mother, how understanding she was
when I got divorced, or else I want to stop caring.
Meanwhile, my mother masters forgetting: which
museum she means to visit, the name of the play
she saw yesterday, what day it is today.

This is the year I intend to excavate my terror,
melt down my resentment, blow it into molten
orange glass, shape it into a shining sculpture
of one enormous woman and cool it and smash it.

My mother has become tiny and pathetic and brave.
Recently she has learned *thank you* or even *please*.
She lives in her elegant house like a black pearl
from a broken oyster drifting under reefs in a bay.
She lives in her house like a startled rabbit unable
to finish crossing the road. If I had enough pity,
I would dare to squeeze her fragile neck and kiss
her forehead as I press down on her windpipe and keep
on pressing with my strong and generous thumbs.

2.

These days my mother surprises me, slowed,
gentled, taking trees into account.

It's not what I'm used to, this appreciation,
watching the squirrels scamper up black bark
like acrobats of joy, while the long afternoon
withdraws into twilight, her mechanical tide
of oxygen yawing through waves and troughs
of breathlessness.

This drowning old lady is not my mother. Not
abrupt. As I stroke her knuckles, grace glints
in our salt hands.

Spring Housecleaning

I am sorting through a cupboard of skeletons:
the giving flesh I used to touch has fallen away,
the pretty boy whose smell I breathed for lunch.

I am sorting through odd drawers of notions:
a hundred, hundred tiny silver thimbles stashed,
or what is prophesied by seeing thirteen crows.

But mostly today I am sorting through words:
everything shabby or chipped or out-of-date
gets set on a table for my coming garage sale.

There you have *soup tureen, concupiscence,
insurmountable grief.* Here you have *bobeche*
for catching candle drips, *pianoforte, shame.*

I'll bargain: take two, and the third comes free.
I'd meant to set out *pincushion, darning egg,*
but then I couldn't seem to live without them,

just as I still need *williwaw,* that terrible polar
squall.

What I Got

From the bag of hats, topped with an apricot feather.
From the bag of heads, narrow with curly notions.

From the bag of hands, stubby with strong thumbs.
From the bag of knees, noisy with white scars.

From the bag of shoes, slanty with leather wings.
From the bag of loam, blown footprints of the dead.

From the bag of skies, bumptious with whirlwinds.
From the bag of planets, our own with its one moon.

From the bag of universes, the very last one in the bag.
And now I am shaking the bag inside out:

> No reader, no poem, no bag. Nowhere,
> my sweetie-pies, to abide.

My Hobo Heart

I entered delight like a village
I had never expected to visit;
I plodded uphill into town,
my bindle hanging from a mop
of dirty white strings.

I'd found no delight by the tracks
and none in the click of the crickets,
but I followed the tidy sidewalk
to the corner of School Street and Joy
where seesaws danced up and down.

I knocked on the door of a house
where a woman opened the door
and held out a glass of water;
I drank delight like a cordial
and gave back the empty glass.

I hopped the next freight west
and rattled out of that burg
which wasn't on any map;
when I left delight like a village,
delight left no dust on my boots.

As If I Could Ever Go Home

1. Inventing groceries

As I walked the valley in my torn cape,
I had no pockets and nothing in them,
not even my fists.

I dug with cracked nails into stony soil
for new potatoes, eyeless and tender
under the storm.

The cooks in the castle had fat fingertips
ending in olives or chocolate cherries
to sweeten the tongue.

I carried soaked oats in a grocery sack
until the bag leaked. Then I licked clean
the plate of the rain.

I warmed my babies by a flaming cedar;
I sucked on cinders for dinner
as if they were coins.

And all that while, up there on the hilltop,
yellow lanterns glowed in the castle
like golden butter.

2. The homelessness of the highly imaginative

Nothing under the bridge
belonged to your grandmother.

Your sandals slice
at the sores on your toes.

Inside your cardboard box,
you sketch with a burnt stick:

you draw flowered curtains
and a porcelain plate;

you sit yourself down
on the ground and you feast.

The UN Commission on Refugees: A Radio Interview

Q: What do you do for food?

A: We borrow food

> I say, *No, no new sneakers this week*
> I say to my children, *Because I said so*

Q: Have you ever returned the food that you borrowed?

A: No

> I tell my kids, *Because we can't afford them*

Q: What do you do when you don't have food?

A: We drink water to fill our stomachs

> and I whisper, *Sweet dreams*

Q: What do you do when you don't have water?

A: We stop crying and start walking
   until we see the safe blue trucks

A: We say, *Do you see guns?*

A: We say, *Mama,*
   or we say, *We have no mama*

> or else we have mislaid
> our magical voices
>
> so that we speak only
> with the worms in our toes

Incidental Music for the 6:00 pm News

Cowbells collect the evening. We are pulled
to the bare kitchen bulb like large moths,
while milking-shed cats curl into straw.

At a rosewood table in a paneled room
middle-aged men in wide leather chairs
sip twenty-year-old single-malt scotch.

Under the white kitchen light
clover honey melts into biscuits;
nobody is starving; nobody weeps.

The men in their nail-studded armchairs
caress their knuckles and nod their chins,
quite certain they have never been wrong.

The chorus of cowbells *ka-bong rattle-rattle*,
the chorus of crystal shot glasses set down,
chorus of moths beating powdered wings,

while out by the bins behind the Club
a woman who stole one sharpened pencil
is carving this song into her skin.

A Question of Class

An orange chair and a skinny chicken
must indicate something, just like a man
with a goat and a guitar. The Dilly sisters

who squat at the end of a long dirt lane
are pure post-structuralists. In their flypaper
shack, *A plus B* equals *A plus B*

which, if you were to ask the Dilly sisters,
is entirely different from *B plus A*,
but nobody thinks to ask the Dilly sisters.

The goat-man sat in their orange chair
plucking his guitar. He was waiting for soup;
men like him are always waiting for soup.

It's a question of class and expensive teeth,
just like it's always been. Women like me
have white poodles groomed for kissing.

Suppose I make soup from the squashes
I've hoarded for beauty in a Tuscan bowl;
still and all, I know that the goat-man

won't show up to sing in *my* house.

So let me tell you,

it was fun being a respected skunk,
and I've always looked good in stripes.
But this latest incarnation? Forget it:

a woman who goes to the dentist
to hear that her fillings are cracked,
who dreams about sorting socks?

I'd rather come back as a narwhal
prodding the ice with my one long tooth
whose ivory spirals spell multiple lives.

My life as a vulture was something else:
carrion for breakfast, carrion for lunch,
nothing to recommend it but the soaring.

So maybe you think I'm making this up?
Maybe you haven't yet been a whelk or
a mouse or a brown pelican;

or maybe you're so busy sorting socks,
you have only the wet thoughts of a worm
bleaching on a sidewalk after the rain.

Worm, Worm, are you wearing your saddle,
that pink citellum that wraps your middle,
that almost fibrous belt of flesh

ready to hoist you up and up
into the changeable Book of Shapes?
I am.

Moral Accounting: A Song Cycle

1. I Exactly Remember Being Fifteen

To throw myself naked into the snow,
to burn in the beaded cold,
to know belly and breasts and thighs,
to sense the moon on my back,

to rise up out of the snow,
to dump myself into ironed sheets,
to be warm and then wet
as if I were small and had peed the bed:

it was everything I would ever learn
about sex and death, completely forbidden,
completely true, one stop on my way home.

> If Mother had found me I would have been shamed,
> if Daddy had found me I would have been judged:
> Why was our lawn so much like an ocean?
> How was I already so ready to drown?

2. Ghost

As if I returned from out of the green sea
and my great grandmother were casting her net
and her flukes were woven from foam

There's no going back to veiled grandmothers
or the seal-fur mother who left me with the maid
or even the daughter I dragged under waves

Tonight I could clamber onto the barnacled dock
squeezing a sea urchin in one punctured hand
I could punish my tongue with needles and salt

3. Penance

    —for a short boy I jilted

All these years later you are a splinter in memory,
one minor figure in a crowd scene surrounding a saint

where I am the sin-stricken donor kneeling in the corner,
or I am a gilded spider dawdling from a rafter who falls
forever on my own silken cord into a pit. No. No, you
are the long rebuke like an icicle and when you melt

to nothing, there is a hole in my soul through which
any lost traveler might contemplate the farthest star.

4. Her Motto: *Never Surprised*

She would have liked to feel outrage,
but everything she grieved for
had happened on each continent
and was certain to happen again.

Each March white trilliums
sprang from the bones of the earth
and slowly pinkened and slowly shriveled.
For recreation, she straightened her spine.

5. The Decor of Eroticism

is not what you think, not the erogenous zones, not brandy;
no, it's sunflower husks after a thrush, or moss on a twig,
an orange light rising at the coast range, dusk in the valley,
what pulls your belly to the verge of bursting, the startled rush
that shivers and shivers and ends, what even fishes
are gifted to know.

6. Survival

Today a hummingbird flew against the window;
I mistook its beak for the stem of a curled leaf.

I have quaffed nectar for all of my life
and my ten knuckles are lovely and white

under the creping skin of my hands.

7. Oppositions

—for my ex-husband whose feet were amputated

When I was little, it seemed so easy:
the opposite of vanilla was chocolate;
the opposite of pepper was salt.
Now the opposite of my big toe going forward
is my other big toe stepping ahead of it.
I know I am lucky to have two souls:

the child-soul who trusts my feet to go on
together, and also the Manichaean soul
who has reckoned amputation.

Your skin was gathered like a stitched parcel,
and, under the blind white of the bindings,
glowed the slick and corded crescent of scar.

Sometimes the opposite of reach is chair.
Sometimes the opposite of love is pity.
Sometimes the opposite of loss is loss.

8. The Song I May Be Called Upon to Write

When the DJ phones from the local a.m. station and says,
The world is about to end; do you have any comment?
I will have to stand up, I will have to sing:

> *Gloria, gloria, gloria,*
> *the heat of a baby's head in my palm,*
> *the intoxication of lilacs,*
>
> *even the madness of murder,*
> *blood as a brown crust*
> *on the blades of the onion grass,*
>
> *to have cared about anything that much—*
> *the human flame in the guts*
> *or coarse white hair of a mountain goat*
>
> *caught in the gorse.*

The one song.

Malingering in the Cellar of Grief

A white poinsettia from last Christmas rests
under cellar stairs in the dust of nutmeg.

Everything needs its dark sleep.
Back in the cobwebs, its papery leaves

glow green, each leaf-point tending down
to the gray basement floor.

Today I will water my sorrow. I tip out water
through the wide rose of the watering can.

I'm so busy enjoying how the doodad
with its spaced holes is called a rose

that the whole watering can empties itself
out and the crusted flowerpot brims over.

If I were a prisoner here, I'd lick the floor.
A blind mutter of voices: She is and she does.

Do you suppose this one bleached leaf
will snap off?

Or do you suppose, wherever it is they hide
from us,

that our dead can get thirsty?

How Do I Grieve for You?

In my house by the garden gate,
I'm weaving a broom out of violets.

In this shed in the midst of the meadow,
I'm braiding a broom out of weeds.

From the white of Queen Anne's lace,
I tat my veil.

You who have gone forth,
I think you linger in the birch tree—

your dark eyes in the white bark
keep watching me sweep.

Backwards and forward,
I lift and lower my two beautiful brooms.

I could go on sweeping for years,
and your absence would still be here

sifting like dust about my wrinkled feet.

Eclipse

Earth's shadow sliding over the moon:
suppose I hadn't understood?

The great dragon sipping the light? Or just
the end of the world?

This is the world that ends over and over and then
goes on without us, our tiny smudge of time.

I once sang a ballad for a whole summer
to the velvet folds in my baby's arms: *Croon, croon.*

In my time, said the old lady,
the moon was redder, and men more beautiful.

Perhaps they were. Now
I am that old lady wrapped in perspective

like the sequined veil on my grandmother's hat.
And look, the moon over the cemetery

slowly coming back.

Daily Phone Call to My Mother

What she told me on Thursday:

You can bring your dog
I love every dog that comes
I love the flowers
I love the rain on the terrace
I love the Buddha
I'm loved by everyone who comes around
and I love everybody

My vocabulary is not what it used to be
I think I'm in the way

What she said today:

Isn't it wonderful
all the wonderful years
so many beautiful things
the white lilies

It's so hard to become old and so old
I should hurry up and die and get out of the way

Okay, I'm going to eat now

And what she may say or not tomorrow:

How Death Intends to Instruct

As the red-tailed hawk loves the white-footed mouse
as the hunter loves bear scat clotted with hair
as the stunted oaks, the dry escarpment . . .

The shadow of the hawk is another hawk
someone along the trail behind me
on lavish and muffling moss
Must I turn my face?

I am pregnant with my mother's death

I grow great with her decline. When shall I be delivered?
I'll be there tomorrow, I say on the phone. She's amazed
when I arrive. *Have you met my aide?* she asks politely,
the same kind aide she's had for months.

She remembers to worry, *Do you need more blankets?*
Her radio loud in the airless house, the oxygen machine
humming and spitting as she curls on a waterproof pad.
Oooh, she moans in her sleep, *Ooh, I'm sorry. Ooooh,*

thank you. I love you. I'm sorry. I love you. Ooooh.
I wake her. A gradual smile blooms. *I'm embarrassed*,
she laughs, *to be such a bag of bones.* Her shrunken
skeleton kicks at my heart and inside my belly.

I'm the luckiest woman in the world, she tells me again,
I'm the luckiest woman in the world. Or else she says,
I'm the loveliest woman in the world, and doesn't notice
any difference. She touches my cheek.

This is something new in our shared lives, how she turns
so gentle. I labor hard with her. Forgiveness loosens
my stubborn bones. I am swollen with her love for me.
When shall I be delivered?

Riding to Lluriac

Darkness pulls me to the wetlands of Lluriac
and other countries inside my head.

I don't want to miss any thing, I don't;
not the chisel gone from the locked box,

none of my tangible objects of beauty,
the zebrawood vortex I left in the nook,

the stone kneeler, hands over her eyes.
I was so protective of this house

and the art of collecting, I confused the rich
with the lucky, so nobody guessed

how all that had fallen to me
had been wrung from my own bones.

I wish I had stolen two tall horses
and called out to you, *Ride with me.*

I would have accepted
the sleeping and the waking,

the field of red tatters
and the black wing flattened on the road.

A Woman Painter

On the bank of a river without a name
she is awakened by a dream
of white butterflies.

Vervet monkeys who live in her jungle
have learned to speak in words:
they chutter at snakes

or at transparent eyelids of crocodiles,
bulbous eyes level with the water,
and the water opaque.

Can this woman paint the suspense
of decay? That one green
that is no green?

Nowhere in my unabridged dictionary
does there exist any word
to name this color,

unless the real words are tourmaline
or citrine or soft putrescence
or mossy cellar door.

In the Voice of My Mother Who Wants to Die Faster

Her script insists on snare drums and tambourines,
not this plinking piano draped in mulberry lace:

Girl, what have I raised you for?

Stab me now with the sword of last compassion—
one hundred hand-tufted knots on the scabbard
and peridot at the hilt. Smother me under
shot silk.

Wash my corpse with l'eau sauvage; *dress my hair*
with oil of lime; fasten my traveling cloak
with a turquoise cabochon clasp.

Read me a goodbye story.
Read me this story.
Now close the white door.

Key

Last night I buried a key and lay
flat on the lawn, one ear pressed
to the loose-packed dirt. I listened to time
rusting. Just at the blue start of dawn
when the line between *past* and *now*
stretches most translucent, I rolled onto
my back to stare at my raised bare knees.

I'm sorry to be scolded by squads of jays,
by bushy squirrels who oppose intrusion.
I've always valued the esteem of beasts.
What men think of me is something else:
I used to worry. Now I lie here in grass
for a whole night. No one comes to me
but small creatures, creatures of lawn

and meadow, a screech owl swooping
and one doe who huffled in darkness
and stepped away. How does the key
feel underground? Does it miss a door?
I no longer care where I put that key.
All my life, people have been telling me
how a woman is meant to unlock her body.

Understory

The meadow in which I was born:
> rustled with bees,
> had a corridor straight to the sun,
> gazed back at me as if I were an object
> surrendered for pawn.

The forest where I will die:
> considers its understory daily,
> is slippery with mushrooms
> and twisting snakes,
> repeats and repeats,
> stumbles back after fire,
> wears drooping silver mosses,
> tends always to the possible.

Over my bones, I hope to collect:
> excelsior from a white cedar,
> one noiseless feather of a barred owl,
> delicate toe prints of an orange-bellied newt
> most highly renowned for its poison.

Sacrament of the Moths

Dust from a moth's wing is lint from a prayer.
In a vault in the Vatican, they collect that lint.

The Vatical Vault of Sacred Moth Lint
opens second Tuesdays from three until six.

Lines of the pious spit-shine their coins
as they wait to kneel upon sanctified lint.

The tonsured Father who samples the lint
reports that it tastes of flute. He also tests

bicycles, beatitude by beatitude. *This chain*,
he intones, *hath snagged another angel*.

You've heard him: he pedals through dusk
as if it were moth gauze, dinging his final

crepuscular bell.

About the Author

Penelope Scambly Schott is the author of a novel, six previous poetry books, and five chapbooks. Her poetry books include three historical verse narratives, *Penelope: The Story of the Half-Scalped Woman*, *The Pest Maiden: A Story of Lobotomy*, and *A is for Anne: Mistress Hutchinson Disturbs the Commonwealth* (Oregon Book Award for Poetry, 2008), as well as three lyric collections, *The Perfect Mother* (Violet Reed Hass Prize, 1994), *Baiting the Void* (Orphic Prize, 2005), and *May the Generations Die in the Right Order*. She has received four fellowships from the New Jersey Council on the Arts, and residencies at The Fine Arts Work Center, The Vermont Studio Center, and the Wurlitzer Foundation. Penelope lives in Portland, Oregon where she hikes, grades papers, paints, and spoils her family, especially her dog Lily Schott Sweetdog.

Other Recent Titles from Mayapple Press:

Toni Mergentime Levi, *Watching Mother Disappear*, 2009
    Paper, 90 pp, $15.95 plus s&h
    ISBN 978-0932412-836
Conrad Hilberry and Jane Hilberry, *This Awkward Art*, 2009
    Paper, 58 pp, $13.95 plus s&h
    ISBN 978-0932412-829
Chris Green, *Epiphany School*, 2009
    Paper, 66 pp, $14.95 plus s&h
    ISBN 978-0932412-805
Mary Alexandra Agner, *The Doors of the Body*, 2009
    Paper, 36 pp, $12.95 plus s&h
    ISBN 978-0932412-799
Rhoda Stamell, *The Art of Ruin*, 2009
    Paper, 126 pp, $16.95 plus s&h
    ISBN 978-0932412-782
Marion Boyer, *The Clock of the Long Now*, 2009
    Paper, 88 pp, $15.95 plus s&h
    ISBN 978-0932412-775
Tim Mayo, *The Kingdom of Possibilities*, 2009
    Paper, 78 pp, $14.95 plus s&h
    ISBN 978-0932412-768
Allison Joseph, *Voice: Poems*, 2009
    Paper, 36 pp, $12.95 plus s&h
    ISBN 978-0932412-751
Josie Kearns, *The Theory of Everything*, 2009
    Paper, 86 pp, $14.95 plus s&h
    ISBN 978-0932412-744
Eleanor Lerman, *The Blonde on the Train*, 2009
    Paper, 164 pp, $16.95 plus s&h
    ISBN 978-0932412-737
Sophia Rivkin, *The Valise*, 2008
    Paper, 38 pp, $12.95 plus s&h
    ISBN 978-0932412-720
Alice George, *This Must Be the Place*, 2008
    Paper, 48 pp, $12.95 plus s&h
    ISBN 978-0932412-713
Angela Williams, *Live from the Tiki Lounge*, 2008
    Paper, 48 pp, $12.95 plus s&h
    ISBN 978-0932412-706

For a complete catalog of Mayapple Press publications, please visit our website at *www.mayapplepress.com*. Books can be ordered direct from our website with secure on-line payment using PayPal, or by mail (check or money order). Or order through your local bookseller.